THE LIFE YOU CRAVE IS
WAITING

Published by *I Believe in Me Gospel*

The Life You Crave Is Waiting

The Life You Crave Is Waiting

I Believe in Me Gospel

30 Days to Unlock Confidence, Discipline, and the Life You Crave

~Juan Garcia

— Book One of the I Believe in Me Gospel Series

— Published by I Believe in Me Gospel

Published by I Believe in Me Gospel.
This book is part of the *I Believe in Me Gospel Series.*
ISBN: **979-8-9930795-0-9**
Printed in the United States of America.

Dedication

To my parents, whose sacrifices built the foundation I stand on.
To my family, who stood beside me in the hardest times. And to everyone in my life who has ever forced me to see reality as it is — thank you.
You've made me grow, change, and keep moving forward.

———

Acknowledgments

those who challenged me, those who tested me, who revealed the strength I didn't know I had. I thank you.
To every voice, every moment, every obstacle that pushed me to see the truth: this book carries your fingerprints.

Table of Contents

How to Use This Book

This is not a book you rush through.
It's a book you live with.

Here's how to get the most from it:

1.　　　One chapter a day. Each chapter is designed to be short but powerful — about five minutes of reading.

2.　　　Let it sink in. Don't just read — pause. Ask yourself: *How does this apply to me right now?*

3.　　　Morning or night. Start your day with clarity, or end your day with reflection. Pick the rhythm that fits your life.

4.　　　No rules, just return. While 30 days is the path, some chapters will call you back. Listen. Repetition is not failure — it's mastery.

5.　　　Live the words. Reading is the spark. Action is the fire. Do one thing each day that proves to you this isn't just a book — it's your practice.

Preface

There comes a point in life when you realize something uncomfortable: most of the things that control you are invisible. They aren't the job you hate, the person who broke your heart, or the unfair hand you were dealt. They're the small habits of thought and reaction you've repeated so many times that they feel like "just the way you are."

But the truth is: *you're not stuck that way.*

Your brain is not a fixed machine. It's alive, changing, rewiring itself with every choice you make. Science calls it *neuroplasticity* — the ability of your mind to shape itself. Every thought, every reaction, every perspective leaves a mark. You are, quite literally, carving the pathways of your future with the way you live today.

That means this: if you want a different life, you don't always need more money, more opportunities, or more luck. You need different choices. You need new patterns. This book is not a quick motivational boost that fades in a week. It's a practice — thirty days of short, powerful truths that will challenge the way you see yourself and the world. Each day is a seed. If you water it, it grows into a new way of living.

The key is consistency. Don't just read these words — sit with them. Reflect on them. Watch how they show up in your life. The point is not to finish this book; the point is to finish each day changed, even in a small way.

If you give yourself to this process, you won't just read another book — you'll rewire your life. Now let's begin.

Chapter One: Your Reaction Shapes Your Reality More Than the Event Itself

THINK BACK TO THE LAST TIME SOMETHING WENT WRONG. Maybe someone disrespected you. Maybe life hit you with bad news. Maybe the day just slipped out of your control. You felt the sting, the heat, the rush in your chest — and before you could even think, you reacted.

Now be honest with yourself: was it really the event that ruined you, or was it your reaction to it? This is where most people get trapped. They believe their pain comes from the world outside them — from what was said, what was lost, what was done. But if you look closer, you'll see it: the event ended the moment it happened. What stayed alive, what kept you up at night, what twisted inside your chest... was your reaction.

Here's why this matters. Every time you let your reaction run wild, you're handing over your power. You're letting one comment, one mistake, one disappointment rewrite your entire reality. You might not realize it, but that's how you build a life of constant stress — one unchecked reaction at a time.

But imagine this: what if you could pause? What if, instead of exploding, instead of collapsing, instead of letting your mind spin a hundred stories, you chose your response? The power in that moment would be greater than the event itself. Suddenly, you're not the victim of what happened — you're the author of what happens next.

This isn't just theory. It's the difference between two lives. One person gets cut off in traffic and carries the anger into work, snapping at everyone, ruining the day. Another person gets cut off in traffic, takes a breath, and lets it go — arriving calm, unaffected, unshaken. Same event. Two completely different realities.

And this is where you have to face yourself: how many of your "bad days" are just bad reactions stretched out into hours? How many relationships have been scarred, not by what happened, but by how you reacted? How many opportunities have slipped away because you let emotion dictate your choice instead of clarity?

This is not small. This is your life.

If you master this one truth — that your reaction is more powerful than the event — you can shift the direction of everything. Because no one can stop events from happening. But everyone can master their reaction. And once you do, you'll find a freedom most people never know: the freedom to live in control of yourself.
So as you move through today, watch yourself.

Watch the spark before the fire. Notice how quick your reaction wants to take over.

And remember: that tiny gap between what happens and how you respond is where your entire reality is shaped.

Don't hand that over.

Claim it.

Chapter Two: The Way You Speak to Yourself Teaches the World How to Treat You

Listen to the voice in your head right now. You know the one. The one that says, *"I'm not good enough... I'll never change... I always mess things up."* You've lived with that voice so long that it feels normal, almost invisible. But let me ask you something: if a stranger spoke to you the way you speak to yourself, would you tolerate it?
Of course not. You'd cut them out of your life. You'd say,

"I don't deserve that."

But when it's your own voice, you let it run unchecked — every day, every hour, whispering poison into your self-worth.

Here's what most people miss: the way you speak to yourself is training the world on how to treat you. When you disrespect yourself, you unconsciously signal that it's okay for others to do the same. You accept less. You settle. You shrink. And life mirrors it back.

But flip it. Imagine if your inner voice became your ally. Imagine if you walked into every room with a quiet, unshakable confidence because you'd been speaking to yourself with respect all day. Do you

13

know what happens then? People rise to meet you. They sense your value before you even open your mouth. Opportunities open. Relationships improve. Success begins to stick to you — not because you forced it, but because you finally set the standard for how the world is allowed to engage with you.

It starts in the smallest moments. When you catch yourself saying, *"I can't,"* switch it to, *"I'm learning."* When you hear, *"I'm not enough,"* change it to, *"I'm becoming more every day."* At first, it feels fake.

But repetition turns into belief and belief reshapes your reality.

Here's the truth: life doesn't give you what you want, it gives you what you believe you deserve. And your self-talk is the evidence you hand to the universe.
So today, pay attention.

Notice every word you tell yourself, because each one is either building your future or breaking it.

The way you speak to yourself isn't just about you. It's the standard the world learns to follow. And when you raise that standard, the world has no choice but to rise with it.

Chapter Three: Stillness Is Not the Absence of Action, It's the Mastery of It

We live in a world that worships busyness. If you're not moving, posting, hustling, chasing… you're "falling behind." But look closer — have you ever noticed how the most powerful people aren't frantic? They aren't rushing. They aren't scattered. They move slowly, deliberately, like they already know they've won.

That's because stillness isn't weakness. Stillness is control.

Think about the last time you reacted too quickly. You spoke without thinking. You moved without clarity. You made a choice you regretted. That's the cost of mistaking motion for progress. You weren't acting — you were just reacting.

Now picture the opposite: you pause. You breathe. You watch. And instead of doing what your emotions scream at you to do, you wait until the noise clears. Then you act with precision. One move, clean and exact, that changes everything.

That's stillness.

Here's what happens when you master it: doors that were invisible begin to open. People look at you

15

differently. You carry yourself with a presence that says, *"I don't chase — I choose."*

That quiet power makes you magnetic.

Opportunities come to you. Success begins to orbit you, because success is drawn to those who move with intention, not desperation.

Stillness trains you to be the calm center in the middle of life's storms. While everyone else is swept away, you remain steady. And in that steadiness, people trust you, follow you, and depend on you. That's leadership. That's influence.

So practice it.

The next time chaos calls, don't answer right away. Let silence be your shield. Let patience be your weapon. You'll notice how much stronger, how much sharper, how much more powerful you feel when you act from stillness instead of impulse.

And here's the secret: when you master stillness, you don't just control your actions —
you control your future.

Chapter Four: You're Not Behind in Life, You're Just on Your Own Timeline

Be honest. How many times have you scrolled through someone else's life and thought, *"I should be there by now. I'm late. I'm falling behind."* It's like a quiet panic that lives in your chest, whispering that everyone else is running ahead while you're stuck.

But here's the secret: there is no race. There is no universal clock. The timeline you keep comparing yourself to doesn't even exist.

Look closer — some people find their purpose at 18, others at 48. Some people build wealth early, others build wisdom first. Some people meet love young, others meet love after years of loss. And every single one of them was on time — because they were on *their* time.

What feels like a delay is often preparation.

The struggles you've faced, the detours you've taken, the pain you've carried — they weren't wasted. They were shaping you, seasoning you, preparing you for what's yours. The moment it arrives, you'll realize it could never have come sooner. You weren't behind — you were becoming.

17

Here's where the shift happens: the moment you stop running someone else's race, you free yourself to run your own. And when you do that, life stops feeling like pressure and starts feeling like power.

You start to notice your own lane opening. You stop chasing, and you begin arriving.

And that's when success starts to feel effortless.

Opportunities find you because you're not clouded by comparison. Confidence settles in because you finally see yourself clearly. You carry yourself differently because you know — deeply know — that nothing about you is late.

So take this in: you are not behind. You are not missing out. You are right on schedule. And if you live with that belief, every step you take will carry the quiet, magnetic confidence of someone who knows they're exactly where they're supposed to be.

Because you are.

Chapter Five: Peace Isn't Found, It's Built From Within

Most people spend their lives chasing peace. They think it's hiding in the next paycheck, the next relationship, the next milestone. *"Once I get there, I'll finally feel calm."* But you already know how that story ends — every time you arrive, the peace you thought you'd find slips further away. Because peace isn't out there. Peace is built in here.

Think of it like this: every time you let go of something you can't control, you're laying a brick.

Every time you choose patience instead of anger, you're laying another. Every time you forgive, instead of replaying the hurt, you're building walls around yourself that no chaos can break through. Piece by piece, choice by choice, you're constructing a fortress of peace inside you.

Now imagine walking into your day with that kind of foundation. Imagine the world raging around you — deadlines, drama, disappointments — yet inside, you're steady. Calm. Untouchable. People will wonder how you do it. They'll lean on you. They'll respect you. And without realizing it, you'll become magnetic. Because real peace isn't just felt — it's seen. And people are drawn to it.
Here's the secret most never learn: peace is not weakness. It's a power move. When you're calm, you

think clearer. You decide smarter. You attract better. Success sticks to the person who isn't easily shaken, because peace gives you the focus and energy that chaos steals from everyone else.

So today, don't wait for peace to appear. Build it. With every choice you make, every reaction you master, every burden you release, you're stacking bricks. And before long, you'll notice — the peace you were chasing out there has been living inside you all along.

That's when life gets different. That's when success feels lighter. That's when you walk through the world unshaken, untouchable, unbreakable.

Because you built it.

Chapter Six: Your Attention Is Your Greatest Currency

Look closely at where your attention goes each day. Every scroll, every argument, every hour lost in distraction — it's all spending. And the scary part? Most people don't even realize they're going broke. Because attention is not free. It's the most valuable currency you'll ever own.

Think about it: every empire, every company, every influencer is fighting, begging, manipulating for one thing — your attention. Why? Because they know that wherever attention goes, energy flows. And wherever energy flows, reality is built.

Now flip the perspective: if you treated your attention like money, would you still spend it on gossip? On comparing yourself to strangers online? On replaying fears in your head? Or would you start investing it into your growth, your craft, your relationships, your vision?

Here's the shift: the people who succeed are not always smarter, richer, or luckier.

They're the ones who learned to spend their attention wisely. They stopped wasting it on what drains them, and they invested it into what builds them. That's why they look confident. That's why opportunities cling to them.

That's why success seems to orbit their lives.

And you can feel this, can't you? The idea that if you shifted even half the attention you waste into something that mattered… your life would transform. You'd grow faster, create deeper, attract more. You'd walk into every day with the quiet confidence of someone who knows: *I'm not broke anymore. I'm rich in focus.*

So ask yourself today: what will you fund with your attention? Will you bankrupt yourself on noise, or will you build wealth in your future?

Because every second you read this, you're spending. And the way you spend will decide who you become.

Chapter Seven: Your Ego Fears Silence Because Truth Lives There

Notice how uncomfortable silence feels. You sit alone, no music, no phone, no distraction — and suddenly, your mind starts squirming. The ego rushes in with noise: *"Check your messages. Think about tomorrow. Worry about what they said."* It will do anything to keep you from being still.

Why?

Because silence is dangerous to the ego. Silence exposes the truth.

In silence, there's nowhere to hide. The masks you wear, the stories you tell yourself, the excuses you've built — they all start to fall away. And what's left is raw, unfiltered you.

That's why the ego resists it. Because once you see yourself clearly, once you confront what's real, you can no longer be controlled by illusion.

But here's the gift: if you can lean into silence instead of running from it, you discover a power most people never touch. Silence sharpens your mind. It strengthens your intuition. It connects you to clarity that noise always drowns out. And clarity is the birthplace of success.

Think about the leaders you respect. They don't look frantic. They don't fill every moment with chatter. They have presence. And presence comes from comfort in silence. When you master silence, you stop reacting and start directing. You move with authority. You speak with weight. People listen when you finally decide to talk — because silence trains you to carry power without words.

Imagine this: walking into a room, saying less, but commanding more. Making decisions from a calm place that others can't even access. Watching success gravitate toward you because you have something rare — inner stillness.

This is why the ego fears silence — because silence unlocks your truth. And once you have that truth, you are free.

So practice it.

Turn off the noise.

Sit with yourself.

Let the discomfort come, then let it pass.

On the other side is clarity, power, and peace the world cannot shake.

Silence isn't emptiness. Silence is mastery.

Chapter Eight: Every Person You Meet Is a Mirror of You

Think about the last time someone irritated you. Their words hit a nerve, their actions triggered something deep. Maybe you blamed them, told yourself, *"They're the problem."* But pause. What if the only reason it stung was because it touched something inside you — something you haven't faced yet?

Every person you meet is a mirror.

When someone inspires you, they're reflecting back a quality you already have, waiting to be used. When someone frustrates you, they're showing you a wound you haven't healed or a weakness you've ignored. The world isn't attacking you — it's teaching you. And if you pay attention, every encounter becomes a lesson about yourself.

Here's the shift: most people run from mirrors. They avoid the hard truths. They stay blind to their own patterns. And because of that, they repeat the same cycles — in love, in business, in life. But the ones who succeed?

They study the mirror. They take the irritation as a signal, the inspiration as a clue. They use people's reflections to sharpen who they are.

Now picture this: instead of being offended, you're empowered. Instead of reacting, you're reflecting. You start to see patterns in yourself that others can't see. You begin to master them. And slowly, you evolve into someone who can't be easily shaken — someone who grows from everything and everyone.

Do you realize what that means? It means no interaction is wasted. Every person you meet is adding value to your journey, whether they know it or not. And once you live like this, you stop fearing conflict, rejection, or judgment. You start welcoming life as feedback.

That feedback, when mastered, becomes your superpower. It makes you adaptable, wise, magnetic. It makes you someone who attracts success naturally, because you're always learning, always improving, always rising.

So the next time someone bothers you, don't just see them — see yourself. Ask, *"What is this mirror showing me?"* And the more you answer that question, the more unstoppable you'll become.

Because the world doesn't just happen to you. It reflects you.

Chapter Nine: Discomfort Is the Doorway to Growth

Be honest — How often do you avoid discomfort? You skip the conversation, the workout, the challenge, the risk... all because it doesn't feel good. And yet, deep down, you already know: comfort has never made you stronger.
Growth never feels cozy. It burns. It stretches. It demands.

Think of the last time you leveled up in your life. Maybe it was earning a promotion, healing from heartbreak, or pushing your body further than you thought possible. Did it feel easy? Or did it feel like pressure, like resistance, like you were being tested? That's not coincidence — that's the law of growth. Muscles only build under resistance. Diamonds only form under pressure. And you are no different.

Here's what most people don't realize: the discomfort you're running from is the exact doorway to the life you want. On the other side of that hard conversation is respect. On the other side of that extra rep is strength. On the other side of that fear is the success you've been craving.

Now imagine what happens when you stop running. When instead of retreating, you step straight through discomfort. Your confidence grows. Your influence grows. Your opportunities multiply, because people notice when someone can walk into fire without flinching. That kind of presence is rare. That kind of courage is magnetic.

And here's the real payoff: the more you embrace discomfort, the less it controls you. What once felt unbearable becomes fuel. What used to break you begins to build you. And suddenly, you're living in a reality most people will never touch — a reality where you grow stronger with every challenge instead of weaker.

So today, ask yourself: what's the discomfort I've been avoiding? And what if, instead of running, I walked straight through it?

Because behind that door is everything you've been asking for.

Chapter Ten: Gratitude Turns What You Have Into Enough

Think about how often you whisper to yourself: *"If I just had more… if I just had that… if I just got there."* That quiet hunger never stops. And the cruel trick is this: even when you finally get what you want, the feeling of "enough" slips further away.

That's because enough is never found outside of you. Enough is created inside of you. Gratitude is the shift. Gratitude takes what you already have — your body, your breath, your opportunities, your lessons — and multiplies their value.

Gratitude rewires your mind from lack to abundance, from chasing to creating. The moment you practice it, you stop living like a starving beggar in a feast of blessings.

And here's the paradox: the moment you feel you already have enough, life starts giving you more.

Opportunities flow to those who radiate appreciation, because appreciation attracts. The person who's grateful is magnetic, unshakable, powerful. Success sticks to the one who knows how to recognize it, even in small doses.

Now imagine this: waking up tomorrow with nothing in your life changed, but with the eyes of gratitude switched on.
The same house suddenly feels like abundance.

The same relationships feel like gifts.

The same challenges feel like training.

You'd walk lighter, speak differently, carry yourself with the confidence of someone who knows they are already rich — and that wealth multiplies wherever they go.

This isn't blind optimism. This is power. Gratitude doesn't just make you feel better — it makes you *be* better. It sharpens your focus, fuels your energy, strengthens your resilience. It turns the "not enough" that's been draining you into a force that fills you.

So today, stop and count it.

Name what you have.

Breathe it in.

Let yourself feel how much is already yours.

Because the person who lives in gratitude never runs out. They're too busy multiplying.

Chapter Eleven: You Don't See Life As It Is, You See It As You Are

Think about this: two people can walk through the same day. One sees problems, insults, setbacks, and reasons to give up. The other sees lessons, opportunities, blessings, and reasons to keep going. Same day. Same events. Two completely different realities.

So what changed? Not the world. *Them.*

You never see life as it actually is. You see it through the lens of your beliefs, your fears, your expectations, and your past. Your mind is always editing reality — bending it to match who you are on the inside. That means every complaint, every frustration, every limitation you've carried… hasn't come from "life." It's come from the way you've been looking at it.

Now pause and really take this in: if your lens shapes your world, then shifting the lens shifts everything. Change yourself, and the life you see changes with you.

This is why personal growth feels like magic. The moment you expand your mindset, the world looks bigger. The moment you heal, the world looks safer. The moment you believe in yourself, opportunities you never noticed suddenly appear everywhere. They weren't hiding — your eyes just weren't ready.

31

Here's the beauty: when you see differently, you live differently. You make bolder choices. You move with more confidence. You attract people who align with your new vision. It feels like the universe is changing for you, but really, it's you changing for the universe.
And here's the secret taste most people never get: when you upgrade who you are inside, life doesn't just feel lighter — it becomes easier. Success flows smoother.

Relationships deepen.

Challenges shrink.

Why?

Because the world is reflecting back your new self.

So today, stop asking, *"Why is life like this?"* and start asking, *"What lens am I looking through?"*

Because the world you see isn't fixed. It's a mirror. And when you polish the mirror, you'll realize life was brighter all along.

Chapter Twelve: Forgiveness Isn't About Them, It's About Freeing You

Think about the person who hurt you most. Even now, when their name crosses your mind, your chest tightens. Your jaw clenches. Maybe you tell yourself you've "moved on," but in truth, part of you is still carrying it — like a stone in your pocket that weighs you down every single day.

Here's the hard truth: holding on doesn't punish them. It punishes you.

Anger feels like power at first, but it's a chain. Bitterness feels like protection, but it's a prison. And the longer you hold it, the more it drains you — your energy, your peace, your joy, your future.

Forgiveness isn't about letting them off the hook. It's about setting yourself free. It doesn't mean what they did was right. It doesn't mean you forget. It means you decide, *"You don't get to control me anymore. You don't get to live rent-free in my mind."*

And here's where the shift happens: the moment you forgive, you feel lighter. You breathe deeper. Your energy clears. And suddenly, the space that resentment was taking up inside you becomes available — for peace, for love, for opportunity, for success.

Think about it: how much more could you achieve if your mind wasn't replaying old wounds? How much confidence would you carry if you weren't secretly dragging the past behind you? How magnetic would you be if your spirit wasn't weighed down?

Forgiveness unlocks that. Forgiveness is fuel. It's the quiet strength that makes you unstoppable because you're no longer bound to yesterday.

So ask yourself right now: *Who am I still carrying? And how much longer do I want to give them my power?*

The sooner you release them, the sooner you rise.

Forgiveness isn't about them.

It's about you.

It's about freedom.

And freedom is the soil where everything you've ever wanted — peace, love, success — finally has room to grow.

Chapter Thirteen: Your Choices Sculpt the Life You're Living

Look at your life right now — where you are, who you're with, what you feel when you wake up in the morning. It may feel like it all "just happened," like you were swept here by forces outside your control. But if you trace it back, you'll see it clearly: choice by choice, step by step, you built this.

Every yes. Every no. Every moment you stayed. Every moment you walked away. It all added up to *here.*

That realization can sting — because it means you can't keep blaming luck, fate, or other people. But it can also electrify you — because if your past choices built this reality, then your next choices can build a different one.

This is power most people never claim. They waste years waiting for circumstances to change, not realizing the steering wheel has been in their hands the whole time.

Life bends in the direction of your choices. If you choose growth, discipline, focus, gratitude, forgiveness — your reality shifts. Slowly at first, then all at once.

Think about it: how would your life look if, for the next year, you only made choices your future self would thank you for? What if every "no" was a protection of your energy? What if every "yes" was an investment in your vision?

Can you feel the strength of that? Can you imagine the success that would follow you if your choices were aligned with who you truly want to become?

And you can begin now. With the next decision you face, big or small, pause and ask: *"Does this serve the life I want to build, or does it steal from it?"* Then choose boldly.

Choose with vision.

Choose with power.

Every choice you make is a brick. And whether you realize it or not, you're building the house you'll have to live in.

Here's the secret: successful people aren't luckier.

They're choosier. They don't make perfect choices every time, but they make conscious ones. They pause. They weigh. They decide from vision, not from impulse. That's why success seems to "stick" to them.

Chapter Fourteen: Your Beliefs Decide What You Dare to Attempt

Every action you take — or avoid — is chained to one thing: belief. If you believe you're not capable, you won't try. If you believe success is for "other people," you won't step forward. If you believe you're destined to lose, you'll sabotage yourself before the race even starts. And here's the haunting truth: it's not your ability that limits you. It's your belief.

Think of all the times you've said no to an opportunity, not because you couldn't, but because you didn't believe you could. Think of the dreams you've quietly buried because your mind whispered, *"Not you. Not now. Not ever."* Those weren't failures of skill. They were failures of belief.

But here's the shift: belief is not fixed. Belief is built. Every time you push through fear, you strengthen belief. Every time you act in courage, you expand belief. And the stronger your belief becomes, the bigger your choices get, and the bigger your life grows.

Can you feel this? Imagine what your life would look like if your belief in yourself matched your potential. Imagine daring to walk into rooms you once thought were too big, saying yes to opportunities you once thought were out of reach.

People would look at you differently. They'd treat you differently. And success would begin to stick to you, because you'd finally be aligned with what you were capable of all along.

Here's the truth: your beliefs are invisible ceilings. And the moment you decide to raise them, your whole world rises with them.

So today, catch the voice of doubt. Hear it. Confront it.
Then ask yourself: *"What would I do if I truly believed I was capable?"*

And then — do it.
Because the life you dream of isn't waiting on more talent or more luck. It's waiting on more belief.

Chapter Fifteen: The Person You Think You Are Is the Cage You Live In

Who do you tell yourself you are? Maybe you've said: *"I'm not confident. I'm not good with money. I always mess up relationships. I'm just average."* These aren't facts. They're identities you've repeated so many times, they've hardened into walls around you.

And here's the catch: your life never outgrows the person you believe yourself to be.

If you think you're small, you make small choices. If you think you're powerless, you hand your power away. If you think you're destined to fail, you'll find ways to fail — even when success is right in front of you. Not because life demands it… but because your identity does.

But let me ask you this: who told you that story? Where did you learn to shrink? At what moment did you decide to lock yourself in this cage? Because that's all it is — a decision.

And here's the beautiful shift: identity can change. The person you *think* you are doesn't have to be the person you *become.* The walls aren't real — they're beliefs. And the moment you step beyond them, life expands.

39

Imagine walking into tomorrow not as the person you've been, but as the person you want to be. Imagine speaking with authority instead of doubt.

Imagine carrying yourself with the quiet confidence of someone who knows they belong in every room they enter. Can you feel that? That's the power of identity. That's the kind of presence success sticks to — because success is drawn to certainty, and certainty comes from knowing who you are.

So here's your invitation: drop the old story. Release the small cage. Stop rehearsing the limits. And ask yourself: *"Who do I choose to be from this moment forward?"*

Because the person you think you are is optional. And the moment you choose differently, your whole reality changes with you.

Chapter Sixteen: Discipline Is the Silent Bridge Between Dreams and Reality

Everyone has dreams. Everyone has goals. Everyone has a vision of the life they want. But here's the brutal truth: most people will never touch them — not because they weren't smart enough, not because they didn't deserve it, but because they never built the bridge called discipline.

Dreams without discipline are just fantasies. Think about how many times you've started strong — the workout, the project, the habit — only to quit when it got hard, boring, or inconvenient. That gap between starting and quitting is where dreams go to die. And the graveyard is full of people who wanted it… but not enough to keep showing up.

But here's the shift: discipline is not punishment. Discipline is freedom. Every time you do the hard thing when you don't feel like it, you're proving to yourself that you can be trusted. You're strengthening identity. You're stacking confidence.

You're becoming magnetic, because the world respects those who can master themselves. And success? It sticks to discipline. Opportunities flow to the person who shows up consistently, because consistency builds results. Results build credibility. And credibility builds power.

Imagine this: a year from now, your body transformed, your craft sharpened, your money growing — not because of luck, but because every day you made small, disciplined choices your future self now thanks you for.

Imagine walking with the confidence of someone who knows, *"I do what I say. I finish what I start. I can be trusted with greatness."*

That's what discipline gives you.

So today, stop waiting for motivation. Motivation is fleeting. Discipline is eternal. Show up. Even when it's boring. Even when it's uncomfortable. Especially when it's uncomfortable.

Because every act of discipline is a brick in the bridge between where you are and where you dream of being. And the one who keeps laying bricks is the one who eventually walks across.

Chapter Seventeen: Focus Turns Ordinary Effort Into Extraordinary Results

Most people don't fail because they're lazy. They fail because they're scattered. Their energy is spread thin — a little here, a little there — until nothing grows strong enough to break through. Distraction is the silent killer of potential.

But focus? Focus is a weapon.

When you focus, you multiply your power. The same hours that used to disappear into noise suddenly stack into results. What felt impossible before becomes inevitable, because all your energy is no longer leaking — it's concentrated.

Think about the sun. Scattered, its warmth feels nice. But when you take that same light and focus it through a lens, it burns through steel. That's what your mind is like. Scattered, it entertains you. Focused, it makes you unstoppable.

Here's the shift: the most successful people in the world are not the ones doing the most. They're the ones who learned how to shut out distractions and aim their energy at what matters. That's why they rise faster. That's why success sticks to them — because success loves direction.

Now imagine this: instead of juggling ten half-finished goals, you locked onto one mission. You cut out the noise. You poured yourself into it until it became real. Can you feel the power of that? Can you see the confidence you'd carry, the respect you'd command, the opportunities you'd attract — simply because you did what most people can't: you stayed focused?

And here's the best part: the more you practice focus, the sharper it gets. Your mind learns discipline. Your energy learns direction. And suddenly, you're living a life that looks "lucky" to others, but you know it wasn't luck. It was focus.

So today, ask yourself: *What's stealing my attention? What would happen if I cut it out?* Then give yourself permission to go all in.

Because extraordinary results don't come from doing everything. They come from focusing on the right thing — until it bends.

Chapter Eighteen: Patience Is the Secret Weapon That Multiplies Results

We live in a world addicted to speed. Fast money. Overnight success. Instant gratification. And when it doesn't come quick enough, most people quit. They never realize they weren't failing — they were just impatient.

Patience is not weakness. Patience is strength. Think of a seed. You don't plant it today and eat fruit tomorrow. It needs time. Roots must form. Soil must hold. Seasons must pass. And if you keep watering, keep protecting, keep waiting — it breaks through the ground stronger than anything you could have rushed.

Your life works the same way. The habits you're building, the vision you're chasing, the discipline you're practicing — they all need time to compound. And when you cut the process short, you cut your future short.

Here's the shift: success that comes fast often fades fast. Success that comes through patience lasts. Why? Because the process builds you into someone strong enough to hold it. Without patience, you can achieve things you're not yet ready for — and lose them just as quickly.

Now imagine this: while everyone else is quitting at mile two, you're still moving. While others give up when it doesn't pay right away, you keep showing up. And because of that, when your moment comes, you don't just arrive — you dominate. You walk in seasoned, prepared, confident. People look at you and think, *"Where did they come from?"* But you'll know the truth: patience built you.

And here's the taste: patience gives you peace. Instead of panicking about time, you move with calm assurance. Instead of chasing, you attract. And that presence — that unshakable, patient confidence — makes you magnetic.

Success sticks to the one who doesn't rush it, because success trusts patience.

So today, stop asking, *"Why isn't it here yet?"* and start asking, *"Am I still building?"*

Because the ones who master patience don't just win. They keep winning.

Chapter Nineteen: Resilience Turns Setbacks Into Stepping Stones

Life will knock you down. That's not a possibility — it's a guarantee. The question isn't *"Will I fall?"* The question is *"What will I do when I do?"*

Most people stay down. They replay the failure, wear it like a label, and let it define them. But the ones who rise? They're the ones who understand this: resilience is the difference between a failure and a comeback.

Every setback carries two options — stay broken or build stronger. And if you choose resilience, every hit becomes fuel. Every loss becomes training. Every disappointment becomes a stepping stone that lifts you higher than where you started.

Think about the stories you admire. Every champion, every leader, every success story you've ever been inspired by has the same theme: they were broken, but they got back up. And not only did they get back up — they rose sharper, stronger, more unstoppable than before. That's resilience.

Now imagine carrying that energy into your own life. Imagine the power of knowing nothing can destroy you.

That no matter how hard life swings, you'll rise again — and each time, you'll rise bigger. Do you feel the confidence in that? The magnetic aura of someone who cannot be defeated? That's what resilience gives you.

And here's the beauty: resilience makes you fearless. When you know you can't be broken, you stop hesitating. You start daring more, risking more, living bolder. And that's when success finds you, clings to you, sticks to you — because resilience makes you the kind of person success can trust.

So today, when you stumble — and you will — don't ask, *"Why me?"* Ask, *"How can this make me stronger?"* Then rise.

Because resilience doesn't just protect you from loss. It transforms loss into your greatest advantage.

Chapter Twenty: Vision Turns Survival Into Direction

Most people are busy working, hustling, chasing — but if you look closer, they're running in circles. They wake up, go through the motions, collapse at night... and repeat. They're surviving, not living.

Why? Because they don't have vision.

Vision is more than a dream. It's a destination. It's the picture in your mind so clear, so alive, that it pulls you forward even when you're tired, even when you're doubting, even when the world is against you. Vision turns survival into direction.

Without it, you'll keep drifting. With it, every decision becomes sharper. Every yes has weight. Every no has a purpose. Suddenly, your time, your energy, your effort — all of it lines up like arrows pointed at a target. And when that happens, momentum becomes unstoppable.

Now imagine this: waking up each morning not with dread, but with fire. Imagine walking into rooms and people sensing something different in you — the clarity, the certainty, the quiet power of someone who knows exactly where they're going. That's magnetic. That's intoxicating. And that's when opportunities, allies, and success begin to orbit your life.

49

Here's the truth: the world doesn't follow the one who works the hardest. It follows the one who sees the farthest. Vision creates leaders. Vision creates movement. Vision creates gravity.

So today, ask yourself: *What picture am I moving toward? What future do I dare to see?* Don't settle for vague. Get specific.

See it.

Feel it.

Own it.

Because once your vision is alive inside you, the world has no choice but to catch up.

Chapter Twenty-One: Courage Is the Gatekeeper of Every Dream You Have

Think about the dreams you've carried. The book you never wrote. The business you never started. The words you never spoke. The risk you never took. If you trace it back, it wasn't lack of talent that stopped you. It wasn't a lack of time. It wasn't a lack of opportunity.

It was fear.

Fear is the quiet thief of potential. It whispers, *"Not yet. Not you. Not safe."* And most people listen, trading their dreams for comfort. They tell themselves they'll move later, when they're ready. But later never comes. And their life becomes a museum of things they *could* have done.

Courage is the only way out.

Courage doesn't mean the fear disappears. It means you step forward while fear screams in your ear. It means you take the leap, even if your legs are shaking. It means you bet on yourself when nothing is guaranteed. And the moment you do, fear loses its grip.

Here's the shift: every dream you've ever had has one price tag — courage. Pay it, and the door opens. Refuse it, and the door stays locked forever.

51

Now imagine what your life would feel like if you lived with courage. Imagine the opportunities you'd seize, the people you'd meet, the rooms you'd enter, the respect you'd earn. Imagine carrying the glow of someone who no longer flinches at risk, who no longer bows to fear. That kind of courage is magnetic. It draws people in. It makes success stick to you, because success belongs to the bold.

So today, feel the fear — and step anyway. Speak anyway. Try anyway. Move anyway.

Because courage doesn't just change the moment. It changes the course of your entire life.

Chapter Twenty-Two: Failure Is Proof You're In the Game

Most people fear failure like it's death. They avoid it, hide from it, and when it finally comes, they treat it as a final verdict: *"I wasn't good enough."*

But failure isn't an ending. Failure is evidence. It means you dared. It means you tried. It means you stepped into the arena while others stayed safe in the stands. Failure is not proof you're weak. Failure is proof you're alive, you're moving, you're in the game.

Think about it: every person you admire has a trail of failures behind them. Every champion, every innovator, every leader — they all lost more times than most people ever even attempted. But they didn't wear failure as shame. They wore it as training. Every miss taught them aim. Every stumble built their strength. Every fall prepared them to rise higher.

Here's the shift: failure only becomes defeat when you stop. If you keep moving, failure transforms into progress. Each scar becomes proof of resilience. Each lesson becomes a stepping stone. And the more failures you collect, the closer you are to mastery. Now imagine this: instead of shrinking in shame, you wore your failures with pride.

Instead of hiding them, you let them show — as badges of experience, proof of your courage. People would respect you more. Opportunities would trust you more. Success would stick to you more — because the world trusts the one who's been tested and still moves forward.

So today, don't ask, *"What if I fail?"* Ask, *"What will I gain if I do?"* Because every failure carries a gift — wisdom, strength, growth — and those gifts are what carve you into the person success can't ignore.

Failure doesn't end you.

Quitting does.

So fail boldly. Fail often. And keep moving. Because failure isn't the opposite of success — it's the path to it.

Chapter Twenty-Three: Persistence Breaks Down Walls That Talent Alone Cannot

Talent is powerful. Skill is important. But history is filled with talented people who quit, skilled people who stopped, gifted people who gave up too soon.

The difference between those who dream and those who achieve isn't always brilliance. It's persistence. Persistence is showing up again after the "no." It's trying again after the failure. It's staying on the path when the results are invisible. Most people don't fail because they couldn't — they fail because they wouldn't keep going.

Here's the truth: life has walls. Obstacles. Delays. Resistance. And most people hit one wall and turn back. But persistence doesn't turn back. Persistence knocks again, and again, and again — until the wall cracks. Until the door opens. Until the world finally makes room.

Now imagine this: you keep showing up long after the average person would've quit. You become the one who doesn't flinch, doesn't stop, doesn't break.

People begin to notice. Opportunities begin to bend toward you. Success sticks to you — not because you had the smoothest path, but because you refused to leave the path at all.

That's the magnetic energy of persistence. It intimidates obstacles. It wears down resistance. It reshapes the impossible into the inevitable.

So today, when you feel like quitting, pause and remember: persistence is the price that breaks barriers. Every time you push one step further than your comfort zone wants, you're proving to yourself — and the world — that you are unshakable.

Because talent may open doors, but persistence is what keeps them open.

Chapter Twenty-Four: Adaptability Turns Obstacles Into Openings

Most people think persistence means doing the same thing over and over until it works. But here's the problem: if you keep hitting the same wall with the same move, all you'll ever get is a bruised head. Persistence gets you to the door. Adaptability finds the key.

Life will change on you. Plans will fall apart. The path you thought was straight will twist, collapse, and demand something different. Those who resist change break under it. But those who adapt? They bend, adjust, and find a way forward no matter what.

Think of water. It flows around rocks, over mountains, through cracks. Nothing can stop it, because it doesn't insist on one path — it insists on moving forward. That's adaptability. And the one who learns it becomes unstoppable.

Here's the shift: adaptability is not weakness. It's strategy. It's intelligence. It's the ability to see ten moves ahead because you're not married to one way. And that's why adaptable people rise — because while others freeze at setbacks, they pivot. They innovate. They create openings where others see endings.

Now imagine yourself carrying that energy. Imagine walking into any room, any challenge, any setback — and instead of panicking, you adjust. You move with calm confidence while others fall apart. People will trust you. Opportunities will follow you. Success will cling to you, because success belongs to the ones who can move with life instead of against it.

So today, ask yourself: *Am I stuck in one way of seeing, one way of moving, one way of believing? Or am I fluid enough to shift, to bend, to find a new door?*

Because the future doesn't belong to the strongest.

It belongs to the most adaptable.

Chapter Twenty-Five: Mastery of Self Is the Highest Form of Power

Most people think power comes from controlling others. But the truth is, the greatest power you'll ever have is the ability to control yourself.

Look around — how many lives are destroyed because people couldn't master their impulses? Anger ruins relationships. Lust ruins loyalty. Greed ruins empires. Impulse, left unchecked, is the invisible chain keeping people weak.

Self-mastery is the key that breaks it.

When you master yourself, you master your reactions, your habits, your emotions. You stop being a puppet pulled by triggers, and you start becoming the one who decides. That is rare. That is magnetic. That is power.

Here's the shift: self-mastery doesn't make life easier. It makes you stronger. And when you're stronger, life bends differently. You carry a calm authority. People trust you more. Success sticks to you, because success can only rest on the shoulders of someone steady.

Now imagine this: you no longer snap when provoked. You no longer waste weeks lost in distraction. You no longer crumble under pressure.

Instead, you breathe. You focus. You act with intention. Can you feel how unshakable that makes you? Can you feel how much respect, opportunity, and influence would flow to someone who cannot be moved by chaos?

That's the gift of self-mastery. It doesn't just change what you do — it changes who you are. It turns you into someone others look to, follow, and depend on. And it gives you the rarest form of confidence: trust in yourself.

So today, ask yourself: *Am I running my life, or are my impulses running me?* Then choose one place to take back control.

Because the one who masters themselves doesn't just survive the world — they shape it.

Chapter Twenty-Six: Your Energy Speaks Before You Do

Walk into a room and pay attention. Before anyone speaks, before anyone shakes a hand, you already feel it — the energy. Some people drain the space. Some people light it up. And without realizing it, everyone responds.

That's because energy is louder than words. Your energy comes from how you think, how you feel, how you carry yourself. When you're bitter, anxious, or exhausted, it leaks out. People sense it. Opportunities sense it. And without knowing why, doors close. But when your energy is aligned — confident, calm, focused — you don't even have to chase. People lean in. Doors open. Success sticks to you.

Here's the sting: most people throw their energy away. They spend it on arguments, on distractions, on worrying about what they can't control. They bankrupt themselves daily — and then wonder why nothing changes.

But here's the shift: when you guard your energy like treasure, when you spend it only on what builds you, your life transforms. You radiate differently. You attract differently. You move differently.

Now imagine this: walking into any room and people can't quite explain it, but they feel it — your presence. Imagine opportunities flowing to you because your energy speaks success before you open your mouth. Imagine carrying yourself with a magnetic force that others can't ignore. That's the power of energy directed, not wasted.

So today, ask yourself: *Where is my energy going? Am I wasting it, or am I investing it?* Then start cutting leaks and fueling what matters.

Because the truth is, your words may convince — but your energy decides.

Twenty-Seven: Your Environment Shapes You More Than Your Willpower

You may think you're in control, but look around: the people you spend time with, the places you go, the atmosphere you live in — they're all shaping you silently.

Willpower gets drained. Environment doesn't. If you're surrounded by negativity, drama, distraction, and small thinking, it doesn't matter how strong you are. Slowly, it pulls you down. That's why so many people stay stuck — they're trying to build greatness inside a cage that keeps breaking them.

But when you build the right environment?

Everything changes.

Surround yourself with people who challenge you, spaces that inspire you, routines that strengthen you — and growth becomes natural. Success feels less like a fight and more like momentum. Your environment does the heavy lifting for you.

Now imagine this: you wake up in a space that fuels you. You spend your day around people who believe in growth. You move in circles where ambition is normal, not mocked. How different would your confidence feel? How much faster would opportunities stick to you? How much easier would discipline become, simply because your environment pushes you forward instead of pulling you back?

Here's the secret: success doesn't come from being stronger than your environment. It comes from designing one that makes strength automatic.

So today, look around. Who's draining you? What spaces are suffocating you? What habits are keeping you small? And then ask: *What would my life look like if my environment was aligned with my vision?*

Because your environment is either your prison... or your launchpad. And the choice is yours.

Chapter Twenty-Eight: The People Closest to You Decide the Ceiling of Your Life

Look at your circle. The ones you text most, the ones you spend your time with, the ones you share your energy with — they are not neutral. They are either pulling you higher or keeping you small.

And here's the truth most people ignore: you don't rise alone. You rise with your circle.

If your closest people are negative, complacent, or full of excuses, it doesn't matter how motivated you are. Their gravity will drag you down. You'll find yourself shrinking to fit their comfort zone, holding back so you don't "make them feel bad," or doubting yourself because their voices echo louder than your vision.

But when you align with the right people? Everything accelerates.

Surround yourself with those who believe in growth, who celebrate your wins, who hold you accountable when you slack — and suddenly, the climb feels lighter. Your confidence expands. Your standards rise. Opportunities multiply, because aligned connections amplify your energy.

Now imagine this: your circle isn't draining you — it's feeding you. The people closest to you push you to be sharper, bolder, braver. You feel yourself leveling up, simply because your relationships demand it. That's the kind of network success sticks to — because success flows where energy multiplies, not where it leaks.

So today, audit your circle. Who's lifting you? Who's holding you back? And the hardest question: who do you need to release so you can rise?

Because the ceiling of your life is set by the people you allow to stand closest to you.
Choose wisely.

Chapter Twenty-Nine: Purpose Turns Existence Into Impact

Most people live, but few actually live *for something*. They wake up, go through the motions, chase comfort, chase approval, chase money — and yet, even when they get those things, something inside still feels hollow.

Because existence without purpose always feels empty.

Purpose is what makes struggle worth it. It's the fire that turns pain into fuel, setbacks into lessons, effort into impact. Without purpose, life is just survival. With purpose, life becomes legacy.

Here's the shift: purpose doesn't always show up as one grand revelation. Often, it's built in small acts of alignment — choosing the work that matters, using your gifts to serve, following the pull that won't let you go. Piece by piece, clarity forms. And when it does, you stop drifting and start driving.

Now imagine this: waking up with a reason bigger than yourself. Imagine walking into every day with clarity, with fire, with certainty that your actions matter. Imagine the confidence of knowing you're not just chasing — you're building something that will outlive you. That's purpose.

And purpose is magnetic. People feel it. Opportunities trust it. Success sticks to it, because purpose gives success a place to land.

And here's the taste: when you move with purpose, fear shrinks. Distractions fade. Time expands. You're no longer just surviving days — you're shaping them. You're turning existence into impact.

So today, ask yourself: *Why am I really here? What is life asking of me?* The answer doesn't need to be perfect. It just needs to be true.

Because once you find your purpose, everything else finally makes sense.

Chapter Thirty: The Life You Crave Is Already Waiting for the Stronger You

Read this carefully — because this is where everything comes together.

Every lesson you've read in these pages has pointed to one truth: you are not powerless. You never were.

What's been holding you back hasn't been the world. It hasn't been luck. It hasn't even been other people. It's been you — your reactions, your beliefs, your choices, your voice, your discipline.

And that's the best news you'll ever hear. Because if you built the cage, you can tear it down. Think about it: all the success you crave, all the confidence, all the peace, all the love — it isn't hiding out there. It's waiting on the version of you who has the courage to claim it. The stronger you. The bolder you. The self-mastered, focused, resilient you.

The question is not *"Can I have it?"* The question is *"Will I become the person who can hold it?"*

Now imagine this: you've done the work. You've faced your reactions, shifted your self-talk, mastered your discipline, sharpened your focus. You've stepped through discomfort, walked in purpose, and chosen courage over fear. You wake up one morning and realize — you've become unrecognizable. Not because the world suddenly changed, but because *you* did.

That's the euphoria. That's the taste of freedom. That's when success doesn't just visit — it lives with you. Opportunities flow, relationships thrive, peace settles in, and everywhere you go, people can feel it: the gravity of someone who has become everything they were meant to be.

And here's the final secret: nothing in this book was about adding something you don't have. It was about uncovering what's been inside you all along. The keys were always in your hand. Now you know how to use them.

So stand up. Breathe deep. Look at your life with new eyes. And decide — not tomorrow, not later, but now — to live as the stronger you.

Because the life you crave is already waiting. And it's been waiting for you.

Epilogue: The Journey Continues

If you've come this far, pause for a moment and honor yourself. Thirty days ago, these words were only pages. But now they've been lived through you.

Each day, you didn't just read — you practiced. You noticed. You reflected. You shifted. And that's how change begins: one seed at a time.

I want to thank you — not just for reading this book, but for daring to face yourself. It takes courage to hold up a mirror. It takes strength to break old patterns. And if you felt uncomfortable, stretched, challenged along the way — good. That's proof that growth is already happening inside you. But this is not the end. This was only the ignition.

You now hold the keys to shaping your reactions, your focus, your discipline, your vision, your purpose. Each chapter was a door you've opened — but behind each door is a room far deeper than we've yet explored. And that's where we're going next.

The next book in this series will dive into these skills one by one — building them, strengthening them, sharpening them until they're unshakable in you. You'll go beyond insight into mastery. Because this isn't something you read once and put back on a shelf. This is something you live.

So as you close this book, don't close the practice. Carry it with you. Let it echo in your thoughts, your choices, your actions. Pick one skill that spoke loudest to you — maybe it was discipline, or silence, or resilience — and begin developing it now. Live it. Test it. Breathe it.

And when the next part of this journey arrives, you'll be ready. Because you are no longer a passive reader. You are the architect of your life, the master of your reality, the one shaping the future with every step.

Until we meet again — walk boldly, live consciously, and never forget: the life you crave is already waiting for you.

Coming Next

You've opened thirty doors.
You've felt the shift.
You've tasted the strength of becoming the stronger you.

But this was only the beginning. In the next book, we will go deeper. Each truth you've met here —
discipline, focus, resilience, stillness, vision — will be broken open, sharpened, and forged into skills you can master.
Not just wisdom you read... but practices you live.

The Mastery You Crave Is Within
Unlocking Confidence, Focus, and Resilience — One Skill at a Time

This book is coming. Stay awake. Stay ready. Stay becoming.

About The Author

I Believe in Me Gospel is a writer, speaker, and creator devoted to helping people break through illusion, reclaim their inner power, and awaken to who they truly are. His work blends timeless wisdom with direct, practical truths that cut through the noise and speak to the soul. This book is the beginning of a larger series designed not only to inspire — but to transform.

About the Series

The I Believe in Me Gospel Series is a movement disguised as books.
It is designed to cut through noise, strip away false identities, and give readers the tools to live awake. Each volume opens doors of awareness, leading from self-discovery to discipline, from confidence to mastery, from survival to creation.
These are not books to passively read.
They are practices to live.

Author's Note

You are powerful.
By holding this book to the end, you've done something most people never do — you've chosen to step into the unknown and take control of your life.
Many will drift. Many will delay. But you decided.
And that decision alone already sets you apart.
Never forget this: you are not waiting on life.
Life is waiting on you.

A Final Word

If this book moved you, don't let it stop with you. The truths you've unlocked here are seeds that grow faster when planted early.

A young adult who begins this journey now — who learns to master their thoughts, emotions, and habits — will carry that strength for a lifetime. The earlier they wake up, the more powerful their growth will be.

So pass it on. Share it. Review it. Gift it.

Not for me. Not for you.

But for the next generation, who needs these truths more than ever.

The faster they are unlocked, the stronger we all become.

Reader's Practice Guide

Read it again. This book will not be the same the second or third time you read it — because you won't be the same. Each pass reveals a deeper layer.

Daily Mantra

I am awake.
I am aware.
I am not a prisoner of my past.
I am not a victim of my thoughts.
I command my focus.
I master my emotions.
I build my future.
Every breath is power.
Every choice is creation.
Every moment is mine.
I am becoming.
I am unshakable.
I am the life I crave.

www.ingramcontent.com/pod-product-compliance
Lightning Source LLC
Chambersburg PA
CBHW071110090426
42737CB00013B/2557